SUPER GROSS ANIMAL PROJECTS

Jessie Alkire

Consulting Editor, Diane Craig, M.A./Reading Specialist

Super Sandcastle

An Imprint of Abdo Publishing
abdobooks.com

ABDOBOOKS.COM

Published by Abdo Publishing, a division of ABDO, PO Box 398166, Minneapolis, Minnesota 55439.
Copyright © 2019 by Abdo Consulting Group, Inc. International copyrights reserved in all countries.
No part of this book may be reproduced in any form without written permission from the publisher.
Super SandCastle™ is a trademark and logo of Abdo Publishing.

Printed in the United States of America, North Mankato, Minnesota

102018
012019

THIS BOOK CONTAINS
RECYCLED MATERIALS

Design and Production: Mighty Media, Inc.
Editor: Megan Borgert-Spaniol
Cover Photographs: Mighty Media, Inc.; Shutterstock
Interior Photographs: iStockphoto; Mighty Media, Inc.; Shutterstock

The following manufacturers/names appearing in this book are trademarks: Anchor®, Crayola®
Model Magic®, Crisco®, Elmer's®, Gedney®, Jell-O®, Morton®, Play-Doh®

Library of Congress Control Number: 2018948856

Publisher's Cataloging-in-Publication Data
Names: Alkire, Jessie, author.
Title: Super gross animal projects / by Jessie Alkire.
Description: Minneapolis, Minnesota : Abdo Publishing, 2019 | Series: Super
    simple super gross science
Identifiers: ISBN 9781532117299 (lib. bdg.) | ISBN 9781532170157 (ebook)
Subjects: LCSH: Animal behavior--Juvenile literature. | Science--Experiments--
    Juvenile literature. | Science--Methodology--Juvenile literature.
Classification: DDC 507.8--dc23

Super SandCastle™ books are created by a team of professional educators, reading specialists, and
content developers around five essential components—phonemic awareness, phonics, vocabulary, text
comprehension, and fluency—to assist young readers as they develop reading skills and strategies and
increase their general knowledge. All books are written, reviewed, and leveled for guided reading and
early reading intervention programs for use in shared, guided, and independent reading and writing
activities to support a balanced approach to literacy instruction.

TO ADULT HELPERS

The projects in this title are fun and simple. There are just a few things to remember to keep kids safe. Some projects require the use of hot objects. Also, kids may be using messy materials, such as glue or food coloring. Make sure they protect their clothes and work surfaces. Review the projects before starting, and be ready to assist when necessary.

KEY SYMBOLS

Watch for this warning symbol in this book. Here is what it means.

HOT!
You will be working with something hot. Get help!

CONTENTS

SUPER GROSS!

There are tons of super gross things in the world. These things can make you feel **disgust**. But did you know this feeling can keep you safe? It stops you from touching or eating things that might be harmful.

Disgusting things can still be fun to think about. That's why many people are **fascinated** by gross things. And animals can be especially gross!

GROSS ANIMALS

Not all animals are cuddly and cute. Some have **slimy** skin. Others have an oily layer of fat called blubber. Many animals stink. And some eat their prey in one **disgusting** bite! Animals can be super gross. But they are pretty cool too!

ALL ABOUT GROSS ANIMALS

Gross animals live all over the world, both on land and in the sea!

NAKED MOLE RATS

Naked mole rats have hardly any hair. This makes it hard for them to stay warm. So, they sleep together in underground **burrows**. Would you like to come across a pile of naked mole rats?

WALRUSES

Walruses and many other **marine** animals have blubber. This is a thick layer of fatty tissue under the skin. Blubber might seem gross, but it keeps sea creatures warm!

COWS

Cows can eat more than 100 pounds (45 kg) of food each day. The grasses cows eat cause gas to build up in their stomachs. Because of this, cows fart a lot!

MATERIALS

FLOUR

PLAY-DOH

BORAX

TOOTHPICK

VINEGAR

AIR-DRY CLAY

SHELLS

COTTON BALLS

PLASTIC FROGS

GREEN CRAFT FOAM

8

PEBBLES OR MARBLES

EGGS

MEASURING CUPS AND SPOONS

FAKE LEAVES OR PLANTS

SALT

FOOD COLORING

LIME JELL-O

SHORTENING

COFFEE GROUNDS

CRAFT GLUE

BLUBBER GLOVE

Observe how oily blubber keeps whales warm!

MATERIALS

- clear plastic container or bucket
- water
- measuring cup
- ice cubes
- spoons
- sealable plastic bags
- shortening

1. Fill a tall, clear container or bucket halfway with water.

2. Add 2 cups of ice cubes to the water.

3. Stir the water and ice. Make sure the water feels icy cold. If it does not, add more ice.

4. Fill a plastic bag about halfway with **shortening**.

5. Put a second plastic bag inside the first bag with the shortening.

Continued on the next page.

6 Stick your hand into the empty inner bag.

7 Use your hand to spread the **shortening** around so the entire inside of the first bag is covered.

8 Fold the top of the inner bag over the top of the outer bag so it stays in place.

9 Stick your hand inside your blubber glove. Then, place your whole glove into the bucket of ice water. How does it feel? Does your hand get cold?

Grossed Out!

Blubber keeps marine creatures warm. It also helps them float in water. Blubber even stores energy in the form of proteins and fats. Animals can live off this energy when food is scarce!

SNAIL SLIME TRAIL

You can make your own snails from Play-Doh and gooey slime!

MATERIALS

- Play-Doh
- shells
- plate
- bowls
- measuring cup and spoon
- craft glue
- water
- spoons
- food coloring
- borax
- non-latex gloves

1. Use Play-Doh to form several snail bodies. They should be long and flat with rounded ends for the heads.

2. Use smaller pieces of Play-Doh to make tiny **tentacles** for your snails.

3. Press the tentacles into the head of each snail body.

4. Press a shell into the center of each snail body.

5. Space the snails apart on a plate. Let the snails sit and set.

6. In one bowl, mix ½ cup of glue and ½ cup of water.

Continued on the next page.

7 Add several drops of green food coloring. Mix well. Add more coloring as needed.

8 In a second bowl, mix ½ cup of water and 1 teaspoon of borax until the borax **dissolves**.

9 Pour the glue and water mixture into the second bowl. Stir to combine everything.

10 With gloves on, knead the mixture with your hands. This will help thicken the **slime**.

11 Pull off small pieces of the slime. Press a piece behind each snail. This is the snail's slime trail!

Grossed Out!

Snail slime is a type of mucus. Snails produce this slime as they move across a surface. The slime protects snails' bodies and helps them move more quickly. It also helps snails stick to vertical surfaces!

STICKY FROG HABITAT

Create a sticky and slimy frog habitat with Jell-O!

MATERIALS

- measuring cup
- water
- large bowl
- 6-ounce box of lime Jell-O powder
- spoon
- pebbles or marbles
- clear glass pan
- fake leaves or plants
- scissors
- green craft foam
- plastic frogs

1   Have an adult boil 2 cups of water.

2   Add the hot water and Jell-O powder to a bowl.

3   Mix well until the powder is completely **dissolved**.

4   Add 2 cups of cold water to the mixture and stir.

5   Scatter pebbles or marbles over the bottom of the clear glass pan.

Continued on the next page.

19

6 Carefully pour the Jell-O mixture around the pebbles or marbles in the pan.

7 Refrigerate the pan for about an hour, or until the Jell-O is halfway set.

8 Once the Jell-O is halfway set, take the pan out of the refrigerator.

9 Press the fake leaves or plants into the Jell-O. They should be suspended in the Jell-O and not sink to the bottom.

10 Place the Jell-O back into the refrigerator until it is fully set.

11 Meanwhile, cut circles from green craft foam. These represent lily pads.

12 Once the Jell-O is set, place the lily pads on top of the Jell-O.

13 Place plastic frogs onto the lily pads to complete your sticky frog **habitat**!

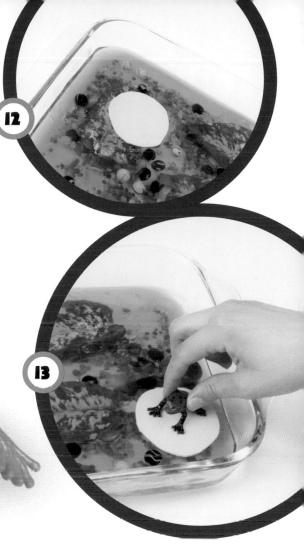

OWL PELLETS

22

MATERIALS

- white air-dry clay
- cotton balls
- markers
- large bowl
- measuring cup
- flour
- salt
- coffee grounds
- spoon
- water
- cookie sheet
- toothpick

1. Use the air-dry clay to make small bones and teeth. Let the clay pieces dry overnight.

2. Meanwhile, color some cotton balls with black, brown, and gray markers.

3. Stretch the cotton balls out and tear them into small pieces. The pieces represent fur.

4. Add 2½ cups of flour to the bowl.

5. Add 1 cup of salt and 1 cup of coffee grounds to the bowl. Mix well.

Continued on the next page.

6. Stir ¾ cup of water into the mixture until well combined.

7. Let the mixture dry out for about 15 minutes.

8. Roll a small ball of the mixture in your hand.

9. Press some clay and cotton pieces into the ball.

10. Add more of the mixture to the ball. Roll the ball so it becomes smooth. This is an owl **pellet!**

11. Repeat steps 8 through 10 to create more owl pellets.

Grossed Out!

Owls can't **digest** certain parts of their prey. These include fur, teeth, bones, and feathers. These parts are pressed into a **pellet** inside an owl's stomach. Then the owl spits up the pellet. Scientists **dissect** owl pellets to find out what owls eat!

12 Leave the **pellets** on a cookie sheet to dry out for several days.

13 Once the pellets are dry, use a toothpick to **dissect** your owl pellets. What do you find?

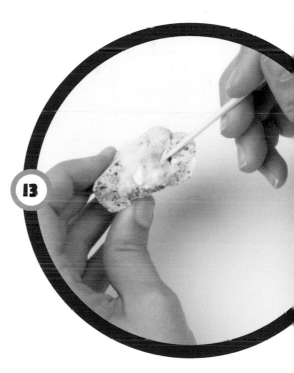

LEATHERY SNAKE EGGS

Use vinegar to make soft, leathery snake eggs!

MATERIALS

- clear plastic cups
- vinegar
- eggs
- spoon

(1) Fill several plastic cups two-thirds full with vinegar.

(2) Add an egg to each cup.

3 Place the cups in a safe spot overnight. The egg shells should **dissolve** in the vinegar.

4 Observe the eggs the next day. Are the shells gone? If not, leave the eggs for a few more hours.

(5) Once the shells are dissolved, carefully remove the eggs from the cups with a spoon.

6 Observe and touch the eggs. Be careful not to break them! How do the eggs feel? What do they look like?

JELLYFISH IN A BOTTLE

You can make a creepy jellyfish out of a shopping bag and some water!

MATERIALS

- plastic shopping bag
- scissors
- measuring cup
- water
- rubber band
- clear plastic container with lid
- food coloring

1 Select a plastic bag. Try to find one with little to no writing on it.

2 Lay the bag flat on a surface. Cut the top and bottom off the bag.

3 Cut both sides of the bag so you have two plastic sheets. Keep one of the sheets.

4 Gather the sheet in between your thumb and pointer finger so a small amount of the sheet pokes up through your fingers. This forms a small head for your jellyfish.

5 Hold the head upside down. Have a helper pour about ¼ cup of water into the head so the head fills up. This will help your jellyfish float.

Continued on the next page.

(6) Twist the plastic bag at the base of the jellyfish's head.

(7) Tie a rubber band several times around the twisted part of the bag. Make sure the water doesn't leak from the bag.

(8) Use a scissors to make many cuts along the bottom of the plastic sheet. These cuts form the jellyfish's **tentacles**. The tentacles should vary in length and size.

9   Fill the plastic container with water. Make sure the mouth of the container is large enough to fit the jellyfish inside.

Grossed Out!

Jellyfish drift along ocean currents. Each has a jellylike body with a mouth in its center. Jellyfish are also known for their long, thin tentacles. The tentacles have stinging cells. These cells can stun or paralyze prey!

10. Add a few drops of blue food coloring to the container.

11. Push the jellyfish headfirst into the container.

12. Tightly twist the lid onto the container.

13. Turn the container over several times to watch your jellyfish drift in the water!

31

GLOSSARY

burrow – a hole or tunnel in the ground that is used for shelter.

digest – to break down food so the body can use it.

disgust – a strong feeling of dislike toward something unpleasant or offensive. Something that gives the feeling of disgust is described as disgusting.

dissect – to separate into parts for the purpose of studying.

dissolve – to become part of a liquid.

fascinate – to interest or charm.

habitat – the area where a person or animal usually lives.

marine – having to do with the sea.

mucus – a slippery, sticky substance produced by the body.

paralyze – to cause a loss of motion or feeling in a part of the body.

pellet – a small, hard ball.

protein – a substance found in all plant and animal cells.

shortening – a fat used as an ingredient in some baked goods.

slimy – resembling or feeling like slime. Slime is a slippery, soft substance.

tentacle – a long, bendable limb on an animal such as a jellyfish, octopus, or squid.